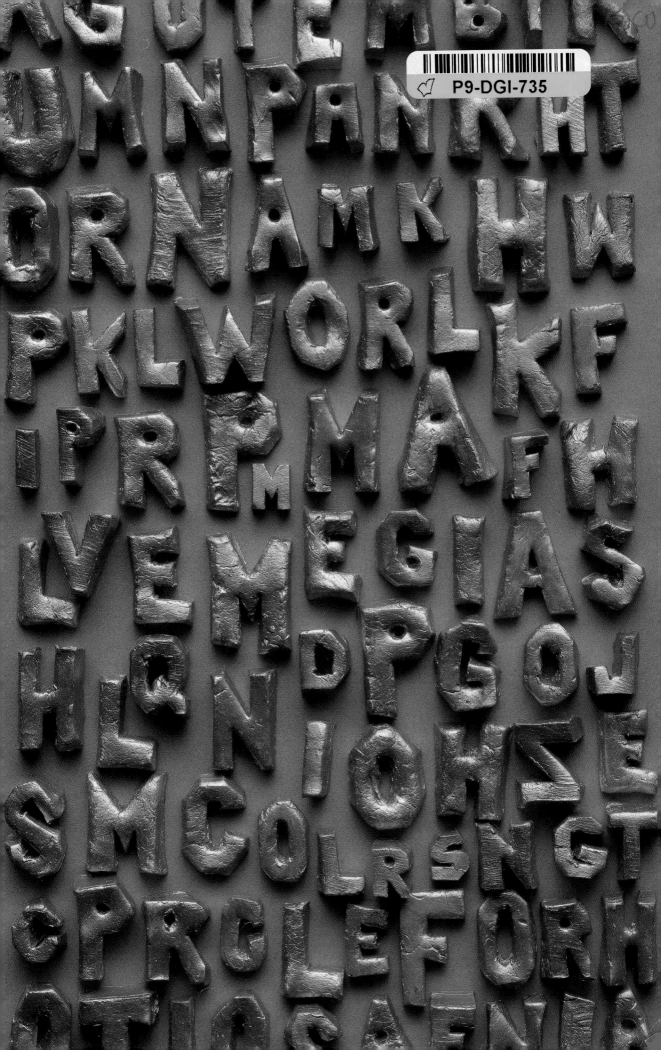

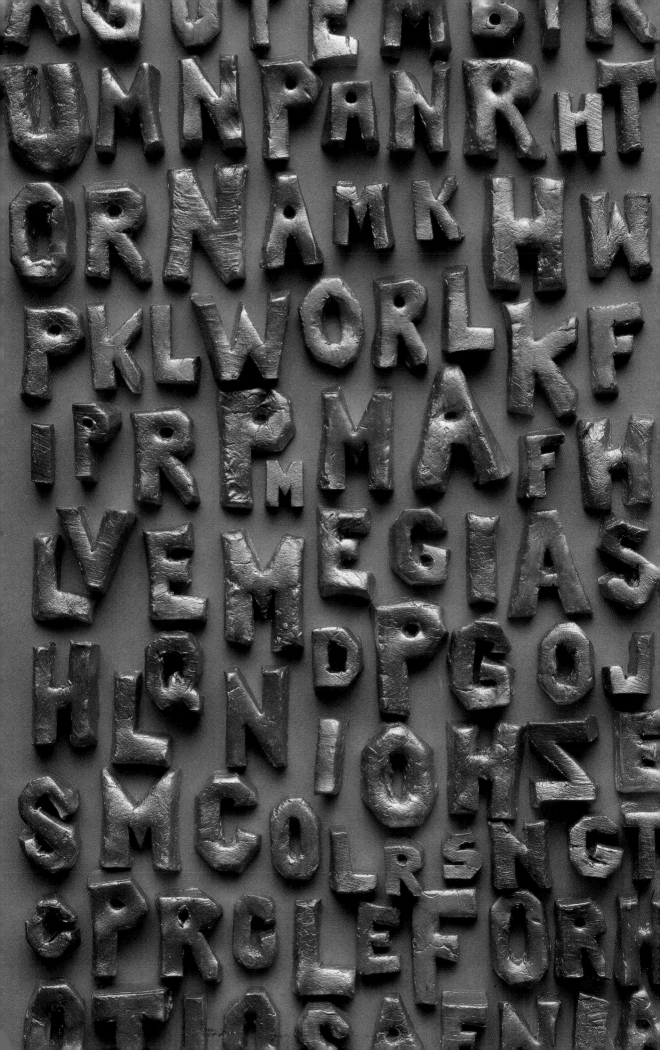

A POCKETFUL OF POEMS

by **NIKKI GRIMES**

illustrated by **JAVAKA STEPTOE**

CLARION BOOKS • NEW YORK

I have a pocketful of words.
I play with them sometimes.
I use them in haiku.
You can borrow most of them
if you want to.

TIANA

The first word is my name.
       T I A N A.
I hang it on a gold chain and wear
it round my neck to keep it close.
Mama says, like me, it's precious.

Tiana must mean
"early bird." My giggles wake
Mama before dawn.

SPRING

Look! Here's a fresh
green growing word.
SPRING. I plant it
like a seed.

6

Mama's window box—

purple flowers shout the news.

Finally—it's spring!

SHOWER

This word wets my pocket.
I have to stay indoors
until my blue jeans dry.
SHOWER is a clean word—
soap and water for the sky.

April showers scrub
the air. No wonder I can
run now. I can breathe!

PIGEON

Ouch! This word pecks at my pocket
like some wild thing, anxious to go free.
P I G E O N.
Its speckled sister paces along
the windowsill, staring in at me.

Pigeons masquerade as wildlife. They can't fool me. We're all city folk.

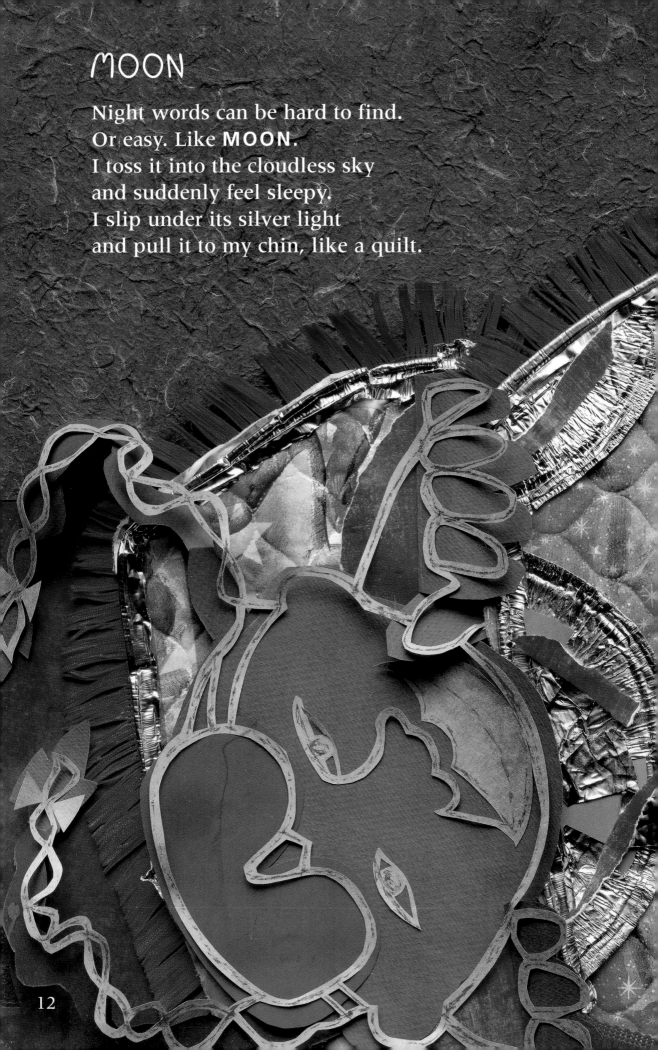

MOON

Night words can be hard to find.
Or easy. Like **MOON**.
I toss it into the cloudless sky
and suddenly feel sleepy.
I slip under its silver light
and pull it to my chin, like a quilt.

Full moon, magic in
silver, speaks to me, drowning
the sound of sirens.

HOT

HOT is a thirsty word that
wakes me from a deep sleep.
I leave my dreams and stumble to the kitchen.
I place the word in the sink, then
turn the cold water on full-blast.

14

Hot days send me to
the water fountain where my
face goes for a swim.

Harlem—July Fourth

fireworks rainbow the night with

bursts of dazzling light

HARLEM

H A R L E M.
What a restless word!
It kicks up its black heels
day and night.
I slide it into my hip pocket
next to AFRICA
and zip it tight.
Daddy says these
are not words to spend
but to save.

CATERPILLAR

The word wriggles in my pocket.
CATERPILLAR.
I reach for it, but it worms away
crawling fast as it can. I get down
on my hands and knees and chase it.

Caterpillar, wait for me. I haven't grown wings yet either. Soon, though!

Labor Day—watch me smash one last homer, take one last sip of summer.

HOMER

Summer words, like *raspberry ice,*
beach, and *barbecue,* are all gone now.
But I find another warm word,
shaped like a bat. **HOMER.**
I wrap my fingers tightly round it
and swing.

20

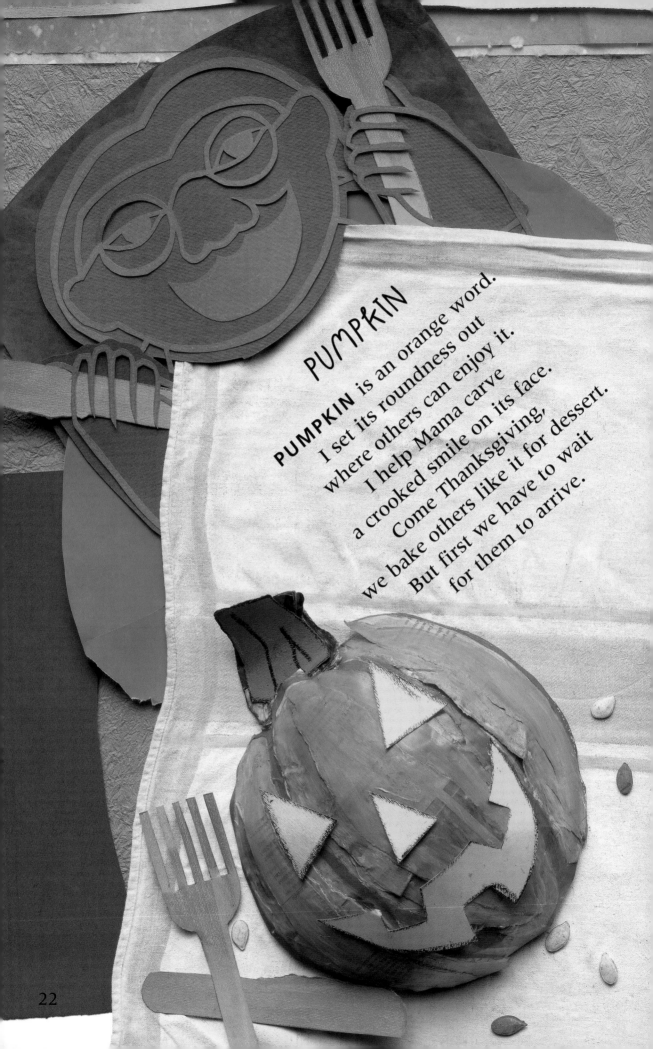

PUMPKIN

PUMPKIN is an orange word.
I set its roundness out
where others can enjoy it.
I help Mama carve
a crooked smile on its face.
Come Thanksgiving,
we bake others like it for dessert.
But first we have to wait
for them to arrive.

Pumpkins catch a bus to town. How else could they get here by Thanksgiving?

SNOW

The word begins to melt
inside my pocket. SNOW.
I fling its lacy coldness
in the air, then watch it
floating there.

24

Magic! Evening snow-
drifts turn each streetlight into
a star on a stick.

ANGELS

Daddy says words have wings
like **ANGELS**—especially the good ones.
In late December, two leap
from the corner of my pocket
and fly.

26

Christmas—one angel
atop the tree, one waiting
below to catch me.

27

GIFT

I turn my pockets inside out.
The only word left is **GIFT**.
I wrestle with the bow
rip away the tissue paper
and find a jeweled box.
Some of the contents spill.
New words for the New Year!
Each one glitters
like my name. Like yours.

Each year is a gift waiting to be opened. Look! This one has your name.

HAIKU

HAIKU. A universe of words
painted on the head of a pin.
I stick it in my silk hatband
so others will notice its beauty.

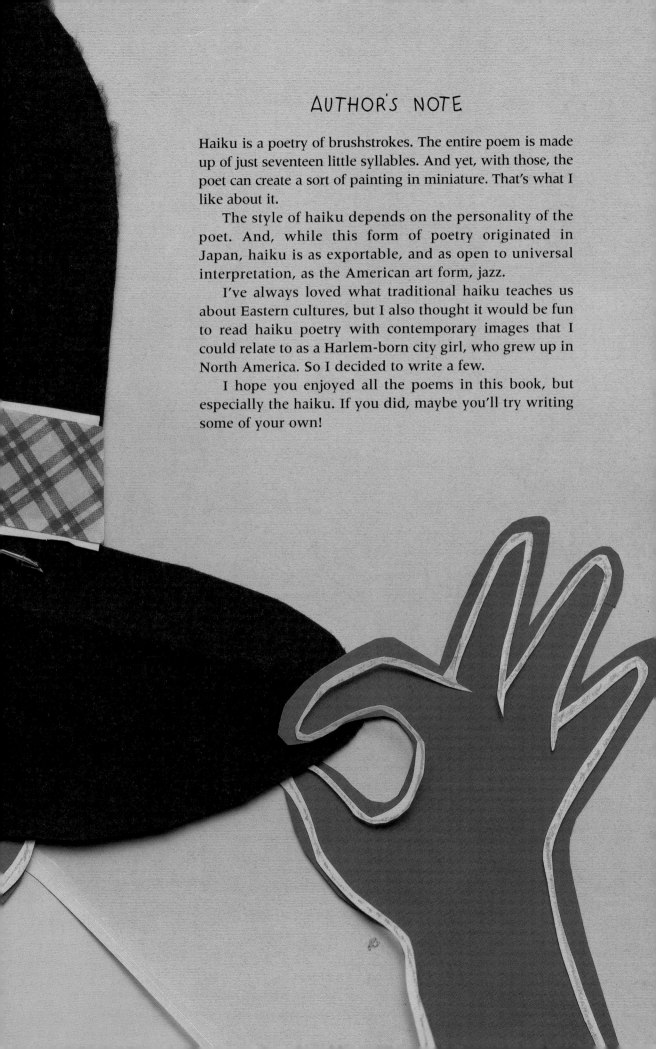

AUTHOR'S NOTE

Haiku is a poetry of brushstrokes. The entire poem is made up of just seventeen little syllables. And yet, with those, the poet can create a sort of painting in miniature. That's what I like about it.

The style of haiku depends on the personality of the poet. And, while this form of poetry originated in Japan, haiku is as exportable, and as open to universal interpretation, as the American art form, jazz.

I've always loved what traditional haiku teaches us about Eastern cultures, but I also thought it would be fun to read haiku poetry with contemporary images that I could relate to as a Harlem-born city girl, who grew up in North America. So I decided to write a few.

I hope you enjoyed all the poems in this book, but especially the haiku. If you did, maybe you'll try writing some of your own!

For Ethan Robert Elisara, future citizen of the planet.
—N. G.

To Mom, Iman, Voice, Bweela, Asha and Ayanna and
Angela. Thank you all for contributing to my life in a
meaningful way.
—J. S.

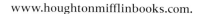

Clarion Books
a Houghton Mifflin Company imprint
215 Park Avenue South, New York, NY 10003
Text copyright © 2001 by Nikki Grimes
Illustrations copyright © 2001 by Javaka Steptoe

Photography of artwork by Gamma One Conversions.

The illustrations were executed in cut paper and found-object collage.
The text was set in 16-point Meridien.

www.houghtonmifflinbooks.com.

Printed in Singapore

Library of Congress Cataloging-in-Publication Data
Grimes, Nikki.
A pocketful of poems / by Nikki Grimes ; illustrated by Javaka Steptoe.
p. cm.
Summary: Poems and haiku verses provide glimpses of life in the city.
ISBN 0-395-93868-6
1. City and town life—Juvenile poetry. 2. Nature—Juvenile poetry.
3. Children's poetry, American. 4. Haiku, American. [1. City and town life—Poetry.
2. American poetry. 3. Haiku.] I. Steptoe, Javaka, 1971– II. Title.

PS3557.R489982 P63 2000
811'.54—dc21
00-024232

TWP 10 9 8 7 6 5 4 3 2 1

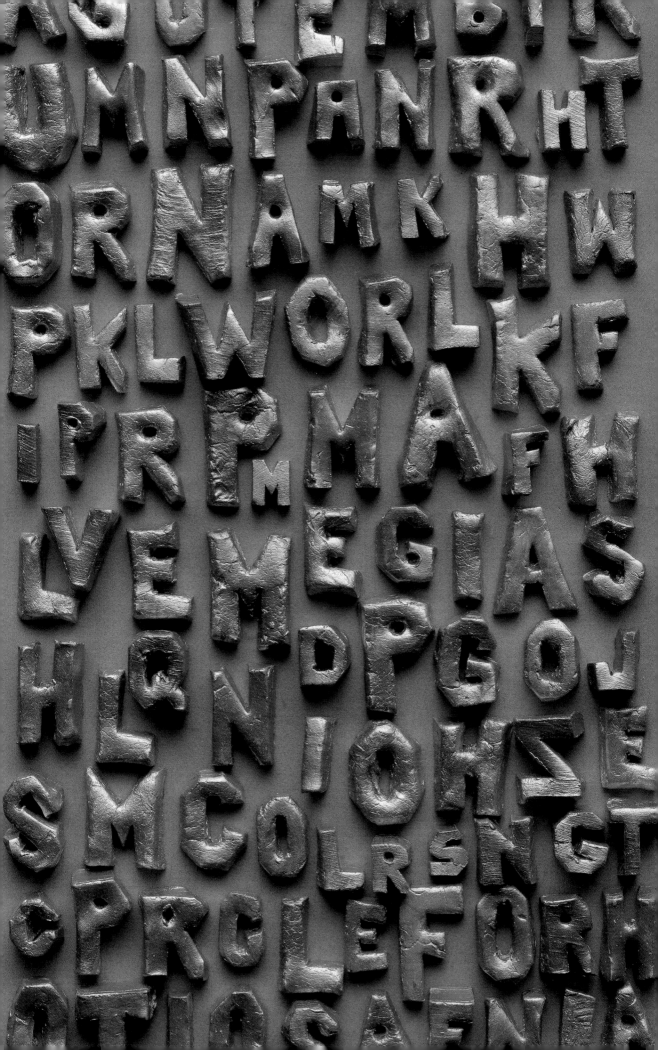